..neth,

The voice of the poor

JI

JI

The Voice of the Poor

John Kenneth Galbraith

The Voice of the Poor

ESSAYS IN ECONOMIC AND POLITICAL PERSUASION

Harvard University Press
Cambridge, Massachusetts, and
London, England   1983

for my onetime and well-loved colleagues
L. K. Jha and B. K. Nehru
and for Mekhala and Fori

Chapter III was the basis for the annual Phi Beta Kappa
Oration at Harvard in 1982. Part of Chapter V appeared in
slightly different form in the *Harvard Business Review,* July/
August 1982.

This book is printed on acid-free paper, and its binding
materials have been chosen for strength and durability.

Library of Congress Cataloging in Publication Data

Galbraith, John Kenneth, 1908–
    The voice of the poor.

    Based on a series of lectures given in India in the spring
of 1982.
    Includes index.
    1. Underdeveloped areas–Addresses, essays, lectures.
I. Title.
HC59.7.G312 1983   330.9172'4   82-18732
ISBN 0-674-94295-7

Preface

*I*N THE SPRING OF 1982, I was invited to India to give the Rajaji Lectures. This is an annual lecture series given traditionally by someone from outside the country under the auspices of the Bharatiya Vidya Bhavan, the great Indian cultural organization. It remembers the wise, diverse, and superbly motivated life (1878–1972) of Chakravarti Rajagopalachari, known affectionately by his countrymen as Rajaji. He was Governor General of India, serving in the years 1948–1950 between Independence and the establishment of the Republic. The Indians accord great warmth of hospitality to their visiting lecturer in an art form in which they are uniquely accomplished, and it was an especially enjoyable return to a land that my wife and I had both learned to love.

As I tell in the introductory first chapter, my theme in these lectures was the relations between the new states and the older industrial lands, socialist and nonsocialist. It is not a topic of high originality, but as a modestly new twist on this familiar thread, I sought to consider the advice which the old countries should be hearing from the new and how, above all, the counsel might be better attuned to the very different stages in historical process in which nations find themselves.

These were lectures, and lectures, I've long felt and previously said, should be heard but never read. On receiving the published speeches of a friend, one should read a few paragraphs at random, react strongly to the opinions of the author, either pro or con, and place them forever aside. Speaking and writing are different forms of expression. The pace of a lecture must be slower than that of the written word; explanations must be more detailed; and various rhetorical devices must be used to get and hold attention. All this is because the listener has no second chance, and once lost, he is gone forever; the reader, in contrast, can always go back and read again. However, in this case, I have extensively rewritten and reduced the original lecture version. What has emerged is, I trust, a reasonably succinct set of essays, which are not, however, without that hortatory and minatory tone a live and attentive audience inevitably invites.

Contents

I
Of Wealth and Wisdom

*T*HERE HAVE BEEN two generally un-
mentioned features that have marked the
intercourse between the older industrialized lands
and the newer countries that became independent
in the years after World War II. The first one, of
less than solemn importance, has been a vast
uncertainty as to how each of these groups should
address the other. It is natural and not undescrip-
tive to refer to the rich countries and the poor; I
here do so. But it is a reference that those who
combine semantic skill with diplomatic tact are at
pains to avoid. There is thought to be something
vaguely derogatory in calling a nation poor, in
spite of the much greater ease of passage of its
people, not in the Christian tradition alone, into
heaven. National poverty in our time can also be
combined with the enormous personal wealth of

some of its citizens from oil. There is even more reluctance to speak about *rich* nations, for with such a description goes an implied question as to whether the enrichment is just or not. Also, perhaps, such a reference carries with it the suggestion of an obligation, inconvenient for some, to help those less fortunate in material well-being.

Thus has come the search for suitable paraphrase. For a time it seemed permissible to speak of developed and undeveloped countries. And, in a more optimistic tone, of developed and developing countries, the latter including some which were visibly receding in economic position. Then came allusion to the Third World, a designation which suffered from the circumstance that almost no one spoke of the First and Second Worlds or, indeed, was quite certain what they were. More recently we have lapsed into geography; the accepted distinction is between North and South. Some factor, still undisclosed, evidently associates wealth and prosperity with the lines of latitude.

All this is foolish and unnecessary; as noted, I shall speak generally in these essays of the rich countries and the poor. However, my purpose will sometimes be more accurately served by referring to the older industrial states and the new nations that came into being in the great era of decolonization that followed the Second World War.

THE SECOND FEATURE of the intercourse has involved not semantics but assumption: it has been taken wholly for granted over the third of a century in which economic development has now been actively under discussion that intelligence in these as in other matters is strongly correlated with income. A country is qualified to extend economic and other advice in accordance with the size of its Gross National Product. The result has been a very large flow of instruction — of counsel, warning, and rebuke — from the rich countries to the poor. There has been relatively little flow in the opposite direction.

It is this second characteristic which sets the mood for these essays. Despite what many consider the best efforts of its own government, the United States is still a notably affluent land. As are Japan and nearly all of Europe, Western and relatively speaking also Eastern. My purpose now is to suggest some of the things which these rich countries should be hearing from the poor. Assuming that the flow of advice and criticism were reversed, that it came in persuasive volume from the poor to the rich, of what would it consist? First I shall deal with economic matters, in particular with the errors of the older industrial powers as regards economic advice and policy and with the neglect of the historical process by which all effective policy must be governed. Then I shall turn to the political relationships between the United States and the Soviet Union on the one hand and the newly independent states on the other; the experience here is rich in meaning for the older industrial powers, capitalist and socialist alike. Next I shall address what I have called the military nexus — the arms competition between the great powers, the flow of weapons to the new states, the resulting tensions, and the consequent grave threat to the survival on this planet of both rich and poor.

The last of my Indian lectures mentioned in the preface reflected the interest of the cosmopolitan business community of the great commercial capital of Bombay. As advice moves from the rich countries to the poor, so do economic effects. It is either good or ill fortune, and in recent times extensively the latter, that much of the world's economic fate is sealed not in local capitals or by the dynamics of local industry and commerce but by what is done in Washington, what happens in the United States. All the world — and in this case specifically India — is understandably interested in the American economic scene; thus the last essay in the series. I would like to think that this essay also includes advice that might flow from the poor lands to the rich, but some will suspect that it is largely advice from the author to the governments of the industrial countries, and more especially to his own. So be it; I would not wholly disagree.

II

The Constraints of Historical Process

*I*N ECONOMIC MATTERS since the end of the Second World War, there has been one point of major agreement between the industrial countries, nonsocialist and socialist alike. And particularly between the United States and the Soviet Union. It is that economic designs reflecting an advanced stage of development can be transferred without appreciable adaptation to the new states of Asia and Africa and, if less specifically, to those of Central and South America. The broad design so transferable and so to be transferred is the one that exists in the originating country. For the Soviet Union that, of course, is socialism, a comprehensive ownership by the state and thus by the people of the means of production and a comprehensive planning of their use. For the United States, with variations derived from individual preference, ideology, or uncertainty, it is a free-enterprise solution. Without denying a certain leadership role to the state and a good deal of public initiative in the development of transportation, power, irrigation, and even basic industry as it is called, the main guidance of the economy should be left to the impersonal operation of the market. The main reliance should be on private initiative sustained and encouraged by private ownership of capital. Both the Soviet Union and the United States have looked at their own plan for economic development, real or assumed, and, as a matter of course, recommended it to others.

On balance, the Americans have been more flexible in their advice than the Soviets, although this cannot be especially ascribed to superior wisdom. It is because we are, by nature, tied less rigidly to a formally articulated economic prescription. Like the other western industrial countries, we have always had more internal debate over what our economic system should be or, indeed, what it is. But in both cases, nonsocialist and socialist, there is broad agreement on exporting the mature domestic product.

And there is another point of agreement. It is believed that economic development — the elaboration of agricultural and industrial plant and equipment — is the sine qua non of national prog-

ress. It comes first; all else follows. From successful agricultural and industrial investment comes
the wherewithal for other, less essential things,
such as a secure political system and universal free
education.

Both the United States and the Soviet Union
have thus united to misunderstand the nature of
national development and to ignore the notion of
historical process that is implicit in the word
development itself. And they have ignored their
own experience.

To put the matter bluntly, there is in all national
development a sequence in which, with much
overlapping, political, cultural, and economic
factors are successively important. The economic
design appropriate to the later stages of development *cannot*, without waste and damage, be
transferred to the early stages. Nor as regards the
new countries can the design and emphasis appropriate to a country in one stage of the political,
cultural, and economic sequence be applied in a
later or earlier stage. What is appropriate for
India, a country relatively advanced in its political
and cultural development, is inappropriate for the
stage in the developmental process that has been
reached by the politically and educationally less
developed states of sub-Sahara Africa or the oil-
producing states of the Middle East. All of this

makes the problem of economic development much more complex than has been imagined during these last thirty-five years, a fact we must accept. The whole question was originally made simple so that it could be accommodated to the ideology and ideologists of capitalism and socialism. Also, perhaps, so that it could be brought within the mental reach of some of those expounding the preferred view of such development.

THE ERROR HERE examined is, to repeat, common to both the advanced capitalist and socialist countries. Both have taken what is appropriate to their own late stage of development and applied it, automatically, to the new nations, which are in the earlier stages. This has been especially serious in the socialist context, for — a less than novel point — socialism requires a large and competent administrative apparatus of high integrity, and in all early stages of political and cultural development such administrative capacity is a scarce resource. It is not even abundantly available in the advanced industrial countries, socialist and capitalist, which now struggle with the unsolved problems of large state and corporate bureaucracies. The essence of all public policy is to economize the scarcest of resources, and this any comprehensive socialist effort in the new countries does not do.

It is something of a puzzle that this has not been better recognized in the socialist world. It was one of the commanding virtues of Marx that he saw all economic life as a process of constant change — of constant transformation. To this end he set much store by the preliminary socializing effect of capitalism, the development of industrial discipline as one of the preparatory steps toward socialism. He would not have taken seriously the idea that socialism could appear suddenly and comprehensively in, say, Mozambique or Ethiopia.

But the failure to see development as a process has been the prime source of error in nonsocialist thinking and advice as well. In the later stages of capitalism all thought on national development and well-being turns automatically to capital investment — to the provision of industrial capital goods, for they are believed to be the means of achieving progress. This belief, in turn, has been basic to the advice and assistance given to the new countries. If you want development, you get solidly ahead with investment in mills and factories, supporting power supply and transportation, the various requisites of modern agricultural production. You may have debate as to sequence and priority in such investment — whether consumer goods or capital goods should come first, with the various choices therein. But investment in plant and equipment is what counts; let there be no soft-headed nonsense on that score. Advocates of socialist patterns of development do not dissent. They believe that hard capital should be socially owned, but it is no less important for progress than in capitalist designs.

However, none of this has been the experience of the older industrial countries, nor has it been the road they themselves followed to their present economic eminence.

In all these countries the early emphasis was not on capital investment but on political and then cultural development. In the United States, Western Europe, and more recently in Japan, a secure political context was stressed in both thought and action on economic development; it was considered the first requisite for economic progress. Were the political system stable and predictable, were it honest and effective, and were there both the sense and the reality of citizen participation, then economic progress was thought to follow. To ensure that it did follow, it was agreed thereafter that education should be compulsory and free and should have as its goal a high standard of basic literacy along with a working sufficiency in the other main branches of learning. No one who recurs to the treatises on economic progress in the last century can doubt the importance then given to a dependable and responsive political structure. Nor can there be any question that a high standard of morality in public affairs was deemed essential for such progress and that popular education was seen as the principal instrument of its achievement.

Modern historiography in the older industrial countries continues to emphasize the political/cultural sequence now so largely ignored in the advice to the new lands. The French Revolution; the American Revolution and the framing and adoption of the Constitution; the Civil War in the American South, with the emancipation of the slaves and the later assertion of civil rights; the unification of Germany under Bismarck; the Meiji Restoration in Japan; the Russian Revolution — all are celebrated for their great ultimate economic effect. Likewise, if less vividly, for the educational surge that always followed.

The literature, even the rigorously economic literature of the last century, does not speak much of capital investment; it was taken for granted, and not too optimistically, that it would appear naturally in a stable political context and with a well-educated population. Only in this century was capital investment seen as the primary instru-

12

ment of progress; it was not that its importance had remained to be discovered, although the development of the national accounts (Gross National Product, National Income) and therewith the measures of its magnitude was certainly a contributing factor. It gained emphasis only as political stability and honesty, popular political participation, and general educational competence were achieved—after these came to be taken more or less for granted.

OF POLITICAL DEVELOPMENT with its associated predictability, efficiency, and integrity as a primary factor in economic development there is little but the obvious to be said. A stable political system accords people the personal security that is the first requisite of economic success. It conveys a sense of political participation, and if the reality of this is less than overwhelming, no propaganda effort is spared to avow it. But political development is indigenous and not something that can usefully be prescribed or guided from the outside.

The importance of political stability in the sequence of development cannot be too strongly emphasized. There is today no country with a stable, participatory, and honest government that does not have—or has not had—a reasonably satisfactory state of economic progress. There are few without such a government of which this can be said.

Special mention must be made of one factor in many of the new countries that is pointedly inimical to effective political development. That is military power. There was a time when armies existed to defend or extend frontiers and to fight wars with neighbors; those objectives have been largely forgotten in numerous of the new countries — a forward step, no doubt. Still, as external defense or aggression has receded in military purpose, internal aggression has advanced. The modern goal of military power over much of the world is to replace the civilian power, dissolve or suspend the often imperfect institutions of democracy, and govern in their place. Latin America is the extreme case of this malign tendency. Constitutional government has been secure in only two countries there in the last fifty years — Costa Rica and Mexico. It is not an accident that in both the army is of negligible importance, and Costa Rica, proudly, has none at all. Durable political institutions do not evolve under military dictatorships; instead there are bred the anger and antagonisms that make government by stable, effective democracy even more difficult.

Much has been written in these last decades of how the poor countries waste resources on their military establishments; of the food, clothing, shelter, and medical care thus denied to the people; and of the civilian capital investment thus forgone. Much, and justly, has also been written on the way in which the industrial powers, through sale or gift, have encouraged this tragedy. The recent report of the Brandt Commission, citing the $14 billion spent externally in 1978 on arms by the countries with the needier peoples of the world, most of it in the United States and the Soviet Union, is eloquent on this subject.[1] But attention needs also to be given to the way these arms expenditures nourish and sustain the major force in opposition to effective democratic political development.

Again the industrial countries should look to their own history. Had Cromwell's generals continued in power in Britain, had military governments remained indefinitely in the southern states after the American Civil War, had Boulanger succeeded in France and established a durable pattern of power, no one can imagine that economic development would have proceeded in those countries as it did. Military sales and aid as now deployed around the world are helping to

1. *North-South: A Program for Survival.* Report of the Independent Commission on International Development Issues (Cambridge, Massachusetts: MIT Press, 1980).

suppress political and therewith economic development; they are burying both under vast quantities of unneeded arms and the soldiers who try with ever-increasing difficulty to understand them but who can, when the opportunity arises, put them to political use. It is a matter to which I shall return.

ON CULTURAL DEVELOPMENT, more specifically education, as a prior requirement in economic development there *is* more to be said. Although the rich countries have, in general, misunderstood their own historical process in this regard, many individuals have not. They have looked at the world and seen one highly obtrusive fact: there is no country with a uniformly literate population that does not have a relatively high and progressive living standard. There is no country with a generally illiterate population that does. Education is not something that economic development affords; it is the experience of the older industrial lands that economic development is what education allows.

Education has also its own inner sequence. In the recent decades of concern for economic development no slight effort has gone into what is called technical training — into the provision of a cadre of men and (some) women capable of the tasks of a higher level of economic attainment. Some of this training was furnished in the schools, colleges, and universities of the older industrial countries; more has required the growth of indigenous institutions. Among the new states India has been, in singular measure, a leader in this effort. One consequence is that India's supply of trained, qualified, and ambitious workers has become the basis for a highly remunerative export, a major reinforcement of her balance of payments.

Important as this technical training has become, it has never had the same standing in development advice as investment in physical plant and equipment; one indication has been the common reference to such cultural activity as "the building of human or social *capital*." It is obvious that nothing can now be considered wholly useful and reputable unless it is given an association with physical capital.

However, technical training is not the first step in cultural development. General education plays an even more vital role,[2] but is at a lower level of modern emphasis.

Poverty, not surprisingly, has its own culture; if it exists and has long existed, people come to

2. A matter to which I have earlier adverted. See *The Nature of Mass Poverty* (Cambridge, Massachusetts: Harvard University Press, 1979).

17

terms with it. They cease to struggle against the obtrusively normal for the seemingly impossible. The world's great religions countenance and encourage such acquiescence. In the Christian tradition only the poor can pass easily into the kingdom of heaven; as the presumptively meek, it is they who, however improbably, inherit the earth. (One is astonished at how many of one's avowedly God-fearing fellow citizens are willing to jeopardize their salvation by the relentless pursuit of wealth and income.) Nothing in the poor lands is more surely wasted than effort and expenditure on economic advance — new agricultural practices, new machinery, industrial guidance, and investment — for people who have accommodated to the culture of poverty. It is the accommodation that must be attacked, and the instrument of this attack is general education. It is this which opens windows through which those caught up in the culture of poverty can look. And so seeing, they are motivated to escape.[3]

3. I am not, as a personal note, drawing this conclusion exclusively from my observation of the Indian or other Asian scene. I grew up among the Scottish clansmen in Canada. Elementary education was then free and compulsory; it reflected the belief that this was the first essential of economic progress. But there were numerous Canadian families that notably and articulately resisted anything more than the most primitive instruction for their off-

The primary case for a prior commitment to education — free, good, and compelled — is that it breaks this accommodation to the culture of poverty. It also has a nexus with democratic government; when one says that democracy requires an enlightened (that is, a literate and informed) citizenry, one gets perilously close to cliché. However, one cannot argue that education always eases the task of government. It allows and encourages a self-assertion and a self-expression which are inconvenient for those who prefer the acquiescence inherent in accommodation — in hopelessness. This difficulty, of course, we cannot regret. And there are politicians in all countries, rich and poor, who rightly sense the importance of popular ignorance for their personal political success. By their very existence, they affirm the case for enlightenment.

Education must never be without a strong commitment, personal and public, to discipline. If

---

spring. They believed, rightly, that it unfitted them for the narrow, hard life of the Ontario farm, that it motivated efforts to escape. They avowed their commitment to the culture of poverty, relative if not absolute, with the words, "It was good enough for my father and so it's good enough for me!" Nothing from my Asian and other experience has led me to doubt the grip in which poverty can hold its people.

we agree that economic development is a worthy thing, then we must agree on the importance of the social sense that it requires from its people and that it requires of them as citizens in their state. One of the most successful cases of economic development in the postcolonial era, and certainly the most improbable, is the city-state of Singapore. That it is a community with a large and energetic sense of citizen participation, none can doubt. I have not joined in the criticism, some of it from my fellow liberals, of the framework of discipline within which that freedom is there exercised. We cannot be casual about liberty, but we can respect an aphorism recited before all graduating classes of Harvard University: there *are* wise restraints that make men free.

Given good general education, the way is open for more sophisticated technical, scientific, or administrative instruction. It is necessary only to stress that it cannot come in isolation from the broad current of educational advance.

Technical education has, in turn, its own sequence — something that came greatly to engage my mind during my years in India. American technicians, abetted by Indian pride, repeatedly urged the most sophisticated as opposed to the most appropriate agricultural and industrial designs. This was true of agriculture in particular.

Were something being done in Kansas, it should be done in Gujarat. Simple and needed guidance on soil and water management, grain hybrids, and fertilizer gave way to complex engineering and social advice, and much effort was wasted in consequence.

Also a seemingly obvious answer where technical skills are lacking is to import them from abroad; let the gap be filled by an infusion of talent from the rich countries. There can, experience shows, be few riskier enterprises. The Russians in China, the Americans in Iran, the Russians in Egypt, the Americans in Indochina have all shown the tensions inherent in such a solution. These tensions are heightened, I shall argue in a later essay, when the ultimate purpose is instruction in advanced military technology. We have here, indeed, one of the most powerful lessons in the relations of the new countries and the old over the last thirty-five years.

THE THOUGHT COULD assail some suspicious minds that in urging the priority of political and cultural development, I am making a case for less aid from the rich countries than in the past. I am not. Cultural and capital development have the same requirements; both call upon the scarce savings of the poor country; both contend with the commanding pressures of current consumption; both, and equally, are made easier or even possible by assistance from the outside.

There are, however, differences in the effect on the rich countries of the various kinds of assistance; there will always be more enthusiasm for help to the poor countries that goes for the purchase and export of physical capital — electric generators, industrial machinery, telecommunications, air traffic control apparatus — than for general grants to help in the building and running of schools. The economic interest of the rich countries is strongly involved in the priority now accorded to capital investment; it is one reason such investment has enjoyed such an unequivocal advantage in the past. We must not, in the future, surrender reality and need to political ease. There are, indeed, countries which have passed through the stages of political and cultural development to the point where capital investment is the prime need. India, though it still has vast educational requirements, is such a case. Generalization is notably the enemy of wisdom where the new states are involved. But no one looking at a good many of the African countries, for example, or the new microstates, as they are called, can doubt the prior importance of schools and teachers and colleges for training more teachers. Again one sees

22

that there are no absolutes; what is right is what is appropriate to the particular stage in the historical process.

I THUS RETURN to my larger point. It is that development *is* a historical process; all prescription must be in keeping with the stage that a country or people has reached in that process. This fact has not been recognized in the flow of recommendation, instruction, and advice from the industrialized world, West and East, capitalist and socialist. The older industrial countries have not taken cognizance of — have not understood — their own history; their recommendations have reflected what is appropriate to the stage of development they have now reached, not what they saw as appropriate in the earlier stages of the historical process — those earlier stages in which the less industrialized or the nonindustrialized countries now find themselves.

One cannot be optimistic that a better historical perception will soon prevail in the rich countries. The assumption is much too strong that what serves or is thought to serve their own development will somehow be appropriate everywhere. And, as noted, so is economic interest. It is important, therefore, that the new countries do not attribute wisdom where it does not exist — that they do not hesitate to challenge the belief that what is currently right for the advanced industrial countries is right for all. They must advise their rich benefactors on how best to help, rather than meekly accepting the well-intentioned if sometimes inapplicable advice they receive. Luckily the essence of their case is conceptually forthright and appealing; at each stop in the long line that stretches from the least developed lands to the most, there is an appropriate design for national development, one that changes as the country in question moves along the line. Recognition of that fact, however, requires specific, objective thought. An effective, stable economic system cannot be established by general formula and certainly not by transferring automatically what is appropriate for the most advanced stages to the least. It would be agreeable, indeed, were economic development so simple; but the experience of the last thirty-five years and more tells us, to our frequent sorrow and frustration, that it is not.

III

The Second Imperial Requiem

I N THE LAST several years there has
been a growing preoccupation the world
over with the threat of nuclear conflict between
the United States and the Soviet Union. It is a
concern I greatly welcome. However, in this
essay I wish to deal with a variant of that issue: the
danger not of direct confrontation between the
two great powers, ominous as that is, but of their
encounter in other countries — the tension and
possible conflict growing out of American and
Soviet imperial ambitions, as they are assumed to
be. I intend to review the history of these imperial
aspirations and to inquire as to the lessons which,
however against instinct, we should draw there-
from. One could wish for a much larger flow of
instruction from the new countries to the old on
these matters, for it is from overlooking the aspi-

rations of the former that the greatest danger comes.

The years following the Second World War were, as previously noted, the great era of decolonization. It is not my purpose here to pass judgment on the earlier exercise of imperial power. Much of what is said on the subject derives far more from emotion than from calm thought refreshed by historical perspective. All things should be judged by the standards of their time; Marx considered British rule in India in his day a progressive force, not for any especially high-minded reason but simply because it was better than the petty, incompetent despotisms it replaced. I once had a lesson from Jawaharlal Nehru on the flexible, matter-of-fact fashion in which this subject should be regarded. I asked him what, in his view, would have been the optimal date for the British to have departed India. He responded with a convincing show of indignation by asking what business they ever had being there in the first place. I reminded him that P. C. Mahalanobis, the noted statistician and a scholar whose credentials as an Indian nationalist were not in doubt, had said that for at least a hundred years the British in Bengal were regarded as liberators. Nehru relaxed, smiled, and said that they should have left after the First World War.

But however one regards the past, there can be no question as to the present. National independence having been achieved, it is fiercely defended in all the erstwhile colonial world. And the sensitivity to anything that has even the appearance of intrusion is very great, as are the political forces that are brought to bear in resistance. There are countries in Africa — Uganda comes especially to mind — where material well-being was higher in the colonial past than it is now. And security in life and liberty was certainly greater. Nowhere, however, does one detect the slightest yearning for the return of imperial rule. The very thought strikes us as eccentric. Yet one comes to the paradox: in the face of this massive commitment to national identity, there continues to be compulsive talk of a new imperialism. Soviet references to American imperialist intention are routine and of long standing; we are, it is held, deeply committed to political, economic, and military domination beyond our borders. And responding allegations from Washington are equally frequent. Early in 1981, President Ronald Reagan was reported as proposing at a Cabinet meeting that the established reference be to the "Soviet Empire," and in later speeches he returned to this usage. Allusion to Soviet "expansionism" is commonplace; as all students of the English language are aware, if something is sufficiently menacing, it becomes an *ism*.

This imperial design of the great powers is thought to be directed at what was the colonial world — the once-subject (or semi-subject) peoples of Central and South America, the Middle East, Africa, and Asia. The motivation is diverse: these former colonies must be saved from Communism; or their people must be liberated from feudalism or the greedy reach of capitalism; or there are strategic concerns — any land with oil or within five hundred miles of an ocean trade route, strait, major port, or the Panama Canal is considered, per se, strategic. Or influence and domination are being sought for their own sake; that is the natural behavior of a great power.

Thus the perception of the modern-day competition for imperial influence. From it comes the danger: in the presumed pursuit of this imperial ambition there could be a collision in some unfortunate land. And terrible consequences would ensue.

But what, in fact, is the nature of this competition? If competition there be, it is the most remarkable ever seen, for no one can look at the history of the last twenty years and conclude that there has been anything but a race to see which of the great powers can lose influence most rapidly.

I HAVE SPOKEN of the period since the Second World War. It is, perhaps, better to begin with the year 1960. The war was then fifteen years in the past; its physical and institutional ravages had been repaired; the postwar pattern of international power and influence seemed firmly established. In that year or a few months later, if I may offer a personal note, I became ambassador to the greatest of the former colonial lands — an agent, surely, of American imperialism. One is allowed one's own benchmarks in citing history.

Twenty years ago, in the aftermath of the war and in the shadow of the military achievements and the political changes that followed, notably in China, there was a certain plausibility in the idea of a new imperialism. One can see how it implanted itself in the minds of those who, occupationally and professionally, are resistant to further thought. In the early 1960s, the seeming imperial domain of Moscow (the flaws being still invisible) was, indeed, impressive. The Soviet Union was clearly the greatest military power in Europe; it was united geographically and in political faith and economic system with China, the foremost military and economic power in Asia. Along the western marches, in turn, was a seemingly faithful band of Communist states — East Germany, Poland, Hungary, Czechoslovakia, Rumania, Bulgaria — as well as the independent but still stolidly Communist state of Yugoslavia and the terra incognita of Albania. To the east and south of China were North Korea and North Vietnam. Such was the vision: an imperium, as it appeared, extending from the Brandenburg Gate in Berlin to the port of Haiphong.

Almost certainly this structure was more impressively solid when viewed from the outside than from within. But this was not known, and it would not have been politically astute to suggest it. Businessmen may, indeed, have gone broke underestimating the intelligence of the American people, but no politician of the time got elected by underestimating the power and unity of the Communist world. All western references were to a Sino-Soviet bloc. Secretary of State Dean Rusk characterized China in those years as a "Soviet Manchukuo" devoid of the essential aspects of sovereignty that would entitle it to membership in the United Nations; all sovereignty belonged to Moscow.

And there was yet more. In Indonesia, Sukarno was backed by a large and powerful Communist party. Egypt, the most influential country of the Arab world, was the recipient of a sizable flow of Soviet arms and advisers. So was Ben Bella in Algeria. There was support to Kwame Nkrumah in Ghana. In Italy and France, Communist parties of size and influence seemed in impeccable subordination to Soviet guidance if not command; the word *Eurocommunism* had not yet been invented. Farther afield, in the new states, socialism and Communism seemed on the wave of the future. Capitalism had not served to break the terrible bonds of poverty; Moscow offered the only and obvious alternative.

TO RECAPTURE THIS PAST is to see the direction and magnitude of the ensuing change: Russia and China now split bitterly apart, the most formidable development of the two decades; Rumania with an independent policy that, on occasion, has involved overtures to Peking; Hungary with its own relatively liberal economic system; Poland, which calls for no current comment; Albania back from an association with China to total ambiguity; various of the western Communist parties, most notably that of Italy, asserting independence; in Indonesia the Communists liquidated with a cruelty that no one anywhere could condone; Russian advisers expelled from Egypt; tanks originally supplied by the Soviets turned against Ben Bella in Algeria to return him to the confinement which, either by the French or by his own people, was his lifetime career; Nkrumah, unwisely absent from his country, ousted. In the new countries socialism, with its dense administrative structure and administrative talent in scant supply, is no longer seen as the glowing alternative to poverty. Given the terrible weight of the latter, one might wish that it were.

Against all this there has been the Communist expansion: to rescue a failing Marxist regime in Afghanistan, a country as inhospitable to imperialism in the last two centuries as any in the world; in Angola, where the MPLA regime is sustained by Cuban soldiers and, in a more practical way, by revenues from Gulf Oil; in Ethiopia, where, as Evelyn Waugh observed, the writ of government has never run reliably much beyond the railroad station (in our day the airport). As a bastion of Communism Ethiopia is in exchange for Somalia, which was an earlier bastion of Communism and is now an outpost of the free world. And there is South Yemen. Such is the twenty-year experience of, as it is called, the Soviet Empire.

LET ME TURN NOW to the American experience. In comparison with that of the Soviets, it is, in some aspects, almost heroic. But it too reveals how insubstantial was the neo-imperialist vision.

Surrounding the vast Sino-Soviet land mass in 1960 were the acronymous expressions of American power—SEATO to the south and east, CENTO in the Middle East, NATO in the west —all of them supplemented by a web of military alliances. In both the treaty organizations and the treaties, the paramount political, financial, and military role of the United States was presumed.

Outside this band of encircling alliances (the word *encirclement* was in common use in those days) lay a community of nations generally friendly to American purposes. From Latin America came strong, even automatic support in the United Nations and the Organization of American States (OAS). Central America and the Caribbean, Cuba apart, were all reliably within the American pale, with only occasional regret over the unduly repellent dictators—Trujillo, the Somozas, Duvalier—who kept them there.

By 1961 it was not possible to muster a secure majority to keep China, as a Soviet province, out of the United Nations. But it was still possible to get the necessary support to have its admission declared an Important Question requiring a two-thirds vote for passage. Only a few years earlier Secretary of State John Foster Dulles had accused those non-Communist countries that stood apart from a formal alliance with the United States of an immoral neutralism. (Even neutrality, if sufficiently deplored, could be an *ism*.) As in the case of Russia, there was then reason to think of an American imperium. And the recent history has been broadly the same.

SEATO and CENTO have gone, more or less literally, with the wind; for it was of wind they largely consisted. Similarly most of the bilateral military arrangements, which assumed that diplomatic and military support could be purchased with weapons and ensured by treaty. The nations so secured would then be our firm allies and stand resolutely against the overtures or threats of the Soviet Union — or China. The reality was that the politicians and governments united under our aegis by these treaties always had enough immediate and pressing problems of their own without being concerned with the seemingly far more theoretical danger from Moscow or Peking. None of the SEATO or CENTO forces would have stood for more than a few hours against a determined movement by the Red Army. The arms were, however, very useful in local wars and for enforcing internal military repression.

The North Atlantic Treaty Organization does, of course, survive. But here, too, as compared with twenty years ago, there is a notably lessened tendency to automatic acceptance of American leadership. On matters ranging from trade policy with the Soviets to missile deployment, negotiation is now required where suggestion would once have served. And negotiation does not necessarily succeed. Nor can we be surprised by this development, for, in our larger policy, we encouraged it. In the years following World War II, we invested thousands of millions of dollars in the industrial rejuvenation of Western Europe, as we also strongly assisted the industrial revival of Japan. The effort, together with that of the countries involved, was brilliantly successful. It was surely to be expected that this achievement would be matched by a similar growth in European and Japanese political self-confidence and self-assertion.

We have also now lost the automatic support of Latin America; no longer do our signals bring from those countries an assured response in the United Nations or the OAS. (The Falklands aberration provides the most recent indication of the muted effect of our voice.) But once again independence was a purpose of our policy. In the sixties we stressed our commitment to our neighbors' economic and political self-determination. And to democracy. That this should have encouraged revolt against oligarchic societies and dictatorial governments in Central America is hardly surprising. We also avowed our commitment to Latin American economic growth and development. That a new industrial power such as Brazil or a relatively affluent member of OPEC such as Venezuela should now assert itself with greater confidence is also to be expected.

THERE HAVE BEEN two unequivocal American reverses in the last twenty years. One of these was in South Vietnam, the other in Iran. Vietnam and Iran were the two new or newly emergent states to which we accorded the closest military and political embrace — in Vietnam an active and costly military participation; in Iran a massive and costly intrusion of financial interest and industrial guidance as well as American military equipment and advisers. In both countries we were brought into association with local leaders, who, in Vietnam, were incompetent and corrupt and, in Iran, oppressive, corrupt, and disdained. In both countries we suffered from the reputation of those we supported. So it will be in the future. The closer the embrace, the worse the result.

The lesson is clear. The will to national independence is the most powerful force in our time. To infringe upon it is to touch the most sensitive of nerves. This has been true for the Soviets; it has been true for us. Respecting that independence, we can have friends; impairing it, we can expect only rejection. If the national leadership is strong, effective, and well regarded, it will not tolerate foreign domination — from anyone. If the leadership is weak, ineffective, unpopular, corrupt, or oppressive, it may accept foreign guidance, support, and a measure of domination, but then it will not be tolerated by its own people. This is the enduring fact of the new imperialism. There are yet other reasons why it is so clearly in retreat.

One of these is that the word *imperialism* itself has been used without regard for its earlier meaning. In foreign policy, as in economics, there is delight in giving substance to shadow, content to myth. What in these last years has been called imperialism bears no close resemblance in fact to the practice of the last century and centuries before. Under the true imperialism the imperial power governed with its own people; it backed that government with its own soldiers or those subject to its discipline. So it was in the Spanish, British, French, and Portuguese empires, in the more exiguous American effort, and, of course, in the great eastern and southern reaches of Imperial Russia.

When this imposed government and military power was weak, it was thrown out; and it did not matter that those so governed were culturally and ethnically identical with their imperial masters. It was Spaniards who threw the Spanish out of New Spain, English who threw the English out of the North American colonies. The instinct for national identity, autonomy, and self-government was already powerfully evident; it is, we must agree, one of the few great constants of modern history. The older imperialism succeeded in suppressing national or ethnic identity only as it brought its authority directly and comprehensively to bear.

The case of India is instructive. The British were enormously aided in conquest, a point mentioned earlier, because they were in comparatively orderly contrast with the anarchic, rapacious, and inefficient despots they displaced. But by the middle of the last century British rule would not have lasted a month in the absence of an effective corps of British administrators backed by British and British-led troops. The mutiny of the Bengal army in 1857 and the prompt collapse of British authority showed everyone where the real source of power lay.

In French, Portuguese, and British Africa power depended similarly on a monopoly of force; the British in Africa expressed it in verse:

> Whatever happens, we have got
> The Maxim gun and they have not.

That is what true imperialism involved. And, in the end, it was not enough. Everywhere contending with the urge for national self-identity, imperialism collapsed. Whatever influence we and the Soviets now continue to have in Western and Eastern Europe is not unrelated to the continuing presence, welcome or otherwise, of armed divisions.

Our attempts to exercise authority in other ways are, by comparison with the older imperialism, a pallid thing. To send in administrators is unthinkable; that would be too obviously reminiscent of an earlier age. At most (and subject to much suspicion) there can be technicians and advisers. Where, as in Afghanistan, Vietnam, and the Dominican Republic, troops were dispatched, this was (or is) deeply against the conscience of the age. Government must, in all cases, be by demonstrably pliable local politicians. This, in turn, as we learned in Vietnam and the Soviets could be discovering in Afghanistan, ensures their discredit. India, in one agitated American view, is much under Soviet influence at the present time. No mentally viable person can imagine that the Indians, having won their independence from the British, would now sacrifice it to the Russians. Were the Soviets suspected of such design, they would be in grave trouble. (I might add that it is hard to imagine any catastrophe for Communism so great as a Communist India.) The threat inherent in our present embrace of Pakistan, the massive arms aid in particular, is not to India (or the Soviet Union); it is to Zia ul-Haq and his government. In accepting our hardware, they will seem too susceptible to our hand. It has long been my feeling, affirmed by some recent reporting,[1] that Cuba would welcome an escape from a too-intimate association with the U.S.S.R. were there a politically and economically acceptable alternative. This alternative we should certainly keep always available.

THERE IS ANOTHER fatal difference from the nineteenth century, one discussed in the last essay. The earlier imperialists were not in the business of exporting or imposing their own social and economic systems; what was found in Asia and Africa was accepted. Trading, mineral, and plantation enterprises were intruded but not with any cultural or ideological motivation. Missionaries did try to alter the local religion, culture, and institutions, and for this very reason there was often friction between them and the colonial adminis-

1. "A Deal with Castro?" by Seweryn Bialer and Alfred Stepan, in *The New York Review of Books,* May 27, 1982.

trators. The latter felt that people should be left to their own sordid social, religious, and other observances and their dubious personal hygiene.

In these last decades great-power influence has had a strong ideological motivation. There is concern to preserve free enterprise or to bring the liberating benefits of socialism. This compulsion is both irrelevant and self-defeating in all early stages of economic development. The choice between capitalism and Communism emerges only after there is capitalism. The most committed ideologist, on walking through a tribal settlement or on viewing a primitive village economy, cannot tell whether it is capitalist or Communist. That is because these simple structures are neither. The effort to impose an economic system does, however, add to the resistance. The evangelists of both free enterprise and socialism are seen as the enemies of established social, cultural, and economic arrangements. This is especially true of socialism; it is the better fortune of free enterprise that it is often whatever happens already to exist. Neither the effort to impose socialism nor the effort to prescribe modern capitalism respects the historical process and sequence outlined in the last essay, a process and sequence that are the essence of political, social, and economic development.

The influence of the United States and that of

the Soviet Union are also diminishing because our economic systems have not, in these last years, been turning in the kind of performance that would make them the lodestar for the rest of the world. Both are highly organized, and both are struggling with the sclerotic tendencies that are inherent in all organizations, public or private, socialist or nonsocialist. But, without question, the main reason for the shared decline of the new imperialism is the unbounded and universal determination of people everywhere to govern themselves.

I HAVE SPOKEN of decline; that is not necessarily synonymous with misfortune. One cannot suppose that in the United States we suffer because we now live in a world of self-confident, self-assertive states. It does less for our national ego, but it could be a useful restraint on ill-considered action. One cannot regret the pressure of our European allies on missile deployment, economic policy, and the use of economic sanctions. Our greatest failure in these last twenty years was in South Vietnam. It is hard to believe that we are economically, politically — or militarily — less well off because that unfortunate peninsula and its calm and pleasant people have been returned to the relative obscurity for which a benevolent nature intended them. The dominoes, Thailand, Malaysia, Singapore — one of the principal cases for our intervention in Indochina — stand as upright as ever. External influence on Vietnam from the Soviet Union, we may be sure, will now encounter the powerful thrust for self-assertion and independence that is inevitable in our time and that, in centuries and decades past, reacted so powerfully in that country against the Chinese, the French, and then ourselves.

The misfortune and danger in these matters lie not in the decline in the external influence of the great powers but in the misperception of its nature. Nations can act dangerously out of an exuberant sense of their own strength. But they can also act dangerously out of the fear of seeming weak. It was such fear that sent us into Vietnam. It was the fear of seeming weak toward a client state that sent the Soviets into Afghanistan. Such fear lies back of the continuing danger in Poland. We must see, as we must hope the Soviets will see, that what is called weakness is, in fact, an accommodation to the realities of our time. The age of imperialism, both old and new, is indeed over. Both for the Soviet Union and for ourselves it has given way to the era of the compulsively independent state. We will fail to recognize this to our peril and our cost.

These are matters on which experience does not compete well with preconception. There is a persistent image of the world divided into spheres of influence—an American orbit, a Soviet orbit. Strategists, telling themselves of their hard-nosed realism, continue to look at a map and assign countries to one great power or the other. Let the rest of us agree that, in the real world, anything that smacks of domination is a two-edged sword which, sooner rather than later, smites those who wield it. In open, supportive association with the poorer countries, the affluent can have a friendly and welcome coexistence. With efforts to guide and dominate, there can only—sooner rather than later—be an adverse response.

Let us recognize and conclude, accordingly, that we are not on a collision course with the Soviets in the new lands unless, in error, we or they will it so. The commitment to national independence is imposing withdrawal on us both. Intrusive action by the Soviets will be primarily damaging to them; intrusive action by us will be primarily damaging to us. That is the experience —the historical process—with which we both contend. Let us pray that we both recognize and respect it. And let it, above all, be the strongly articulated message of the new countries to the old that they are not fit causes for an imperialist confrontation, that they reject domination by either of the great powers and ask only for the same right to self-determination desired by all nations, old and new.

IV

The Military
Nexus

MY CONCERN in the last essay was with the political relationship between the new states and the old, and in particular that between the smaller countries and the superpowers. I now turn to their military relationship, which begins with the somber and, in ultimate effect, comprehensively lethal arms competition between the United States and the Soviet Union. Extending outward from this competition is the effect on the new states as they are swept into this race or are encouraged by the availability of weaponry to cultivate animosities and fears of their own.

The arms culture of the world is, in fact, a four-sided relationship — for anyone with geometric sense, a quadrilateral — standing vertically in the line of vision. At the top of this design, one at each corner, are the United States and the Soviet Union. Across the top, dominating all else, is the continuing weapons competition between the two great powers. Down then from each of them comes a flow of weapons to the new nations grouped at each corner of the base, a flow which is supplemented by weapons from France, Britain, Switzerland, and Israel. Across the base this flow nourishes the antagonisms and sustains the competition between the new countries — countries for which, in many cases, the cost of arms and training in their use is, quite literally, bread and rice from the mouths of their people. It is my intention to address each side of this quadrilateral: the arms competition between the great powers, the flow of weapons by sale or gift from each of them to the poor countries, the competition and tensions thereby inspired.

BY A WIDE MARGIN the most ominous part of this design can be found on the upper line across the top of the rectangle, for there one has the nuclear weapons competition between the superpowers. This, like much in the modern world of arms and armies, is not sustained by any military logic — by anything so obvious as the protection of lives and livelihood or the national survival of those involved. Instead it has a mystique and a dynamic of its own, and they accept as a consequence the likelihood of massive death and the destruction of the very national entities for which the defense is presumed.

There are, of course, many forces perpetuating the arms race; nothing is gained by simplification. One is the technological competition. Each power develops the weapons of ever-greater destructive capacity and precision that render obsolete those of the other. Each, foreseeing such obsolescence, strives to develop those that will, in turn, render those of the other side ineffective and then obsolete. A large and learned community of experts with their own language and values — scientists, engineers, and politicians — nurtures and guides this process.

The technological dynamic is sustained by the economic, bureaucratic, and scientific interest of these specialists — the interest of which President Dwight D. Eisenhower spoke in his best-remembered speech, when he warned on leaving office against "this acquisition of unwarranted influence, whether sought or unsought, by the military-industrial complex." This interest, the bureaucratic interest in particular, cannot be identified specifically with one side or the other. And in both the United States and the Soviet Union it is strongly reinforced by an appeal to fear—fear of what the other side is doing, fear of being thought soft on a potential enemy. In a passage from his memoirs that deserved wider attention than it received, Nikita Khrushchev tells of a conversation at Camp David with President Eisenhower:

> "Tell me, Mr. Khrushchev, [the President asked,] how do you decide the question of funds for military expenses?" Then, before I had a chance to say anything, he said, "Perhaps first I should tell you how it is with us . . .

> "It's like this. My military leaders come to me and say, 'Mr. President, we need such and such a sum for such and such a program . . . If we don't get the funds we need, we'll fall behind the Soviet Union.' So I give in. That's how they wring money out of me. They keep grabbing for more, and I keep giving it to them. Now tell me, how is it with you?"

Here is Khrushchev's reply:

> "It's just the same. Some people from our military department come and say, 'Comrade Khrushchev, look at this! The Americans are developing such and such a system. We could develop the same system, but it would cost such and such.' I tell them there's no money; it's all been allotted already. So they say, 'If we don't get the money we need and if there's a

war, then the enemy will have superiority over us.' So we discuss it some more, and I end up by giving them the money they ask for."[1]

The final and influential force sustaining the weapons competition is the commonly held belief that it safeguards an economic, political, and social system—a way of life. On the American side we are defending free enterprise and free institutions; these are under attack from socialism and Communism; weaponry, whatever the cost and risk, is the means by which we protect them. The Soviet Union, looking out on a predominantly capitalist world, has a reciprocal response. In such manner those committed to a larger social faith—to belief in freedom and free enterprise or socialism and Communism—are swept into support of the weapons race.

If we are to counter the forces that perpetuate it, we must recognize, above all, that the weapons competition does not, in fact, defend social and economic systems, neither that of the United States nor that of the Soviet Union. It is presently putting both systems gravely at risk, the risk of

1. *Khrushchev Remembers* (Boston: Little, Brown, 1970), pp. 519–520. The authenticity of this document, once subject to some challenge, is now generally accepted. There should, of course, be the usual warning about conversations remembered long after the fact.

returning them to a society that far antedates both capitalism and socialism and for which even the words are irrelevant. As always, the historical process. Capitalism and socialism are the highly sophisticated products of this process, and nuclear conflict will have an equally shattering effect on both. Transportation, communications, the food supply, the monetary economy itself will succumb. So also the political institutions of the free world, as well as the even more complex structure required by socialism. Remaining at most on either side will be a medieval economy, unfortunate survivors grubbing hopelessly in the contaminated soil. There will be no freedom, no democracy; these were unknown in the medieval existence not because they had yet to be invented but because in a poverty-ridden context they are irrelevant. None should doubt it; the ashes of capitalism will be indistinguishable by even the most perceptive surviving ideologue from the ashes of Communism.

However, one thing will, indeed, have been accomplished: the differences between the rich countries and the poor will at long last have been eliminated. It is worth reflecting that, by reasonable calculation, the life and well-being of the average citizen of the United States or Russia is even now as much at risk as that of the poorest villager in India. But not even the villager is secure from the dangers of nuclear conflict. The fallout, the ozone effects, the contamination from a full-scale confrontation or from that limited war that some strategic theorists, in a striking immunity to sanity, think possible will, like the rain, come upon the just and the unjust — the innocent and the responsible — alike.

THE TECHNOLOGICAL DYNAMIC in the United States and the Soviet Union must be arrested; the supporting bureaucratic and economic interest must be overcome. Likewise the fear of addressing the problem. By far the most direct and understandable way of doing this is through a bilateral freeze on the development, production, and deployment of further nuclear weapons as the prelude to negotiation on their reduction — and, one hopes, their eventual elimination. The freeze is not impractical, illusory, or visionary; it is a highly sensible, highly practical design for removing the issue from the nearly exclusive control of the nuclear theologians, as they have been called. These are the people for whom the technical and military intricacies involved in the development and deployment of weapons and the policy on arms control negotiation have become an intellectual preserve from which the public, including those urging effective nonsymbolic arms control, are righteously excluded on grounds of ignorance or naiveté. It is a delegation of power, the most fatal in our time, that can no longer be tolerated.

THERE IS, as I have said before, a rising world-wide concern over the dangers of nuclear conflict, an increasing pressure to have that threat nullified and extinguished. It is the strongest of political issues in the United States. No politician would dare speak out directly against this thrust; if resistant to substantive arms control, he must take refuge in the complexities of negotiation from which the public, because it is not fully informed, is excluded. Or he must arouse the fears of Soviet superiority just mentioned. Or he must affirm the need for arms reduction while urging that there should first, for bargaining purposes, be an expansive increase.

The antinuclear political movement extends in its power to Europe and Japan. And, with the Soviets' intimate experience of war, one can hardly doubt its presence in the majestic silences of the U.S.S.R. It is this massive force that must be mobilized behind effective arms control.

There has been much anxiety in recent times over the proliferation of nuclear weapons. It is an anxiety I strongly share; I wish to see them possessed by as few countries as possible and preferably by none. But we cannot assume that there will be safety if these weapons, with their hair-trigger arrangements for release, are possessed solely by the great powers. To every expression of concern for the dangers of proliferation one must ask for a strong voice of assent from all countries, but there must also be a strong demand that, through effective, serious, and nonsymbolic effort on arms control, the great powers reduce the dangers to which they are exposing all the peoples of all the world.

Arms expenditure, we are coming also to realize, is deeply adverse to good economic performance in the older industrial countries and notably in the United States and the Soviet Union. In her useful and authoritative *World Military and Social Expenditures, 1981,* Ruth Leger Sivard concludes:

> Among ten developed countries for which historical data are available [for the years 1960 – 1979], the slowest growth in investment and manufacturing productivity has occurred in two countries (UK and US) where military expenditures are the highest in relation to GNP. The best investment and productivity record is in Japan, where the military-to-GNP ratio has been very low and productivity has grown at an amazing 8 percent per year. [Ger-

54

many with relatively low defense expenditures had also a favorable rate of growth in productivity.]

The poorest record may well be in the Soviet Union, where the proportion of GNP devoted to military programs is higher than in the NATO countries, perhaps twice as high.

She assigns the reasons for the link between costly military effort and productivity:

An arms race . . . drains investment and research resources[,] . . . limits the potential for growth and innovation. On the civilian side, this means an economy less prepared to compete in world markets, less able to provide its citizens with improved conditions of living.[2]

Through the decade of the 1970s the United States used from 5 to 8 percent of Gross National Product for military purposes, while the Germans used between 3 and 4 percent — in most years relatively about half as much. The Japanese in this same period devoted less than 1 percent of their Gross National Product annually to military use. In 1977, to take a fairly typical year, American military spending was $441 per capita; that of

2. Ruth Leger Sivard, *World Military and Social Expenditures, 1981* (Leesburg, Virginia: World Priorities, 1981), p. 19.

Germany, $252 per capita; that of Japan, a mere $47 per capita. It was from the capital so saved and invested that a substantial share of the civilian capital investment came which brought these latter countries to the industrial eminence that now challenges so successfully that of the United States. Again the figures are striking. Through the decade of the seventies American investment in fixed nonmilitary and nonresidential investment ranged from 16.9 percent of Gross National Product to 19.0 percent. That of Germany ranged upward from 20.6 to 26.7 percent. The Japanese range in these years was from 31.0 percent to a towering 36.6 percent. The investment in improvement of civilian plant was broadly the reciprocal of what went for weapons.[3]

So much for the military competition between the great powers — across the top of our rectangle. Now I turn to its bearing on the new states of the postcolonial world.

DOWN EACH SIDE of the quadrilateral from the great powers to the less is the flow of weapons by purchase and gift, a flow that is heavily concentrated on the Middle East, India, Pakistan,

---

3. Figures are from *The Statistical Abstract of the United States* and *International Economic Indicators,* December 1980.

Korea, Libya, and Israel. The 1979 Yearbook of the Stockholm International Peace Research Institute put 1978 arms imports by the new states at $14 billion (in 1975 U.S. dollars).[4] Since then there has been a substantial increase, with a vastly larger increase to come.[5]

From a purely military standpoint, much and perhaps most of this flow is futile, and on occasion bizarre. There is, once more, the fact of historical process. The expensive military hardware so purchased is invariably appropriate to a later as distinct from the current stage of political, social, and economic development of the buyer. In 1982 David Wood of the *Los Angeles Times* told of the problems of the Saudi Arabian defense establishment. It does, indeed, have aircraft. These are F-5s with highly sophisticated F-15s on

4. These weapons came extensively but by no means exclusively from the two great powers. U.S. exports were at $5.8 billion, those of the U.S.S.R. at $4.0 billion. But France supplied $2 billion and Britain and Italy lesser amounts. For a discussion of these figures and the associated policy, see the report of the Brandt Commission, *North-South: A Program for Survival*. Report of the Independent Commission on International Development Issues (Cambridge, Massachusetts: MIT Press, 1980), pp. 117 ff.

5. On the prospective (and massive) United States arms exports, see *The Defense Monitor* (Washington, D.C.: Center for Defense Information), vol. 11, no 3, 1982.

order, as well as C-130 transport planes, helicopters, and also in prospect the much-debated AWACS for surveillance of the desert and surrounding wastes. Only lacking are "the pilots, mechanics, technicians and administrators to make [this] military machine tick." With the precision with which the modern soldier approaches such matters, it is estimated by American military advisers that the Saudi government will not have reached "self-sufficiency" (that is, the ability to dispense with foreigners in the maintenance and operation of its transport aircraft, the F-15s, or the AWACS) until some time early in the twenty-first century. That is truly long-range planning.

Military forces, equipment, and operations must be suitable to the stage of national development of the country that is to use them. Yet again the historical process. We did not suffer in Vietnam because we faced superior technical equipment. On the contrary; if the North Vietnamese and their guerrilla allies had fought with helicopters and supersonic planes and with tanks and armored vehicles, they would not have lasted a month. But consistent with their stage in historical process they moved through the jungle on foot with only the arms, ammunition, and rice rations they could carry. With this we and the much more elaborately equipped forces of the Army of the

Republic of Vietnam could not contend. Israel won its wars with Egypt because it was in harmony with its own relatively advanced weaponry, as the Egyptians were not with theirs. So it was in the conflict between India and China in 1962, a tragedy that I observed at close range. The Chinese, moving over the high mountain passes of NEFA (the North-East Frontier Agency), had weapons in keeping with their time and condition, including their logistical capacity; thus they defeated the more structured and ponderous forces of India.

I would not go so far as to argue that the best way to weaken the military power of a country in the early stages of the historical and industrial process is to hobble it with an array of highly sophisticated equipment — that by such device one diverts men's minds from the lethal instincts of war to the engaging mysteries of modern technology, military administration, and logistics. But there can be no question that much of the arms flow from the great powers to the less is militarily irrelevant.

There is another perverse effect. With the weapons and equipment come the people who instruct in their use and help in their maintenance. Their style of living and public behavior attract attention, as does their association with weaponry and the local military establishment. What are foreigners doing in so sensitive an area? Should there not be suspicion of a malign imperial purpose? What we have seen to be the most responsive of nerves is thus touched. So it was with the Soviet military advisers in China and Egypt and with ours in Indochina and Iran. As a design for alienation, one cannot doubt the efficacy of a large infusion of sophisticated military equipment along with the people necessary for its use.

Still more important is the economic and social effect. These weapons are paid for by the poorest of the poor. This is at cost to civilian investment to raise living standards — at cost, as noted, even to bread itself. And from this privation can come, in turn, the discontent and unrest that react with power and anger against the government, the social and economic system, and the friendly source of arms that is seen as the cause. A further consequence is that the local military power is enhanced in relation to civilian authority. As a result, many more governments in our time have been destabilized by their own armies and arms purchases than have been supported thereby.

ONE COMES FINALLY to the bottom line of the rectangle. From the weapons flow come the resulting tensions and conflict between the recipients — between India and Pakistan, Iran and Iraq, Israel and the Arab lands, between different factions within Lebanon, on the Sahara, in Central America. Much of this is a reflection of the military competition between the great powers, the suspected cultivation by them of allies or acolytes, their dispatch of arms to encourage friends and to support or counter actual or seeming revolutionary thrusts or insurgency.

No one should apologize for being a visionary; without vision, hard-headed (meaning mentally impenetrable) and hopeless men remain without challenge to their lethal tendencies. But one cannot be unduly detached from reality. Men have marched and carried weapons for a long time. And one cannot, alas, urge the complete abolition of armies in the new countries. One can only ask for a fresh and determined look at the problem by those most involved.

I do not minimize the responsibility of the great powers in allowing and, indeed, encouraging the arms flow. But there must now be a stronger counterinitiative from buyers and recipients. These essays have urged a more effective flow of advice from the poor countries to the rich; one must ask for it especially here. It should be made clear to the supplying countries that in the earlier stages in the historical process modern weapons are largely irrelevant. No one should believe that the military wisdom of the great powers is impeccable on this matter, for they will always see their latest (and most expensive) gadgetry as indispensable. They should be made to recognize that this weaponry is frequently, in fact, socially damaging and politically destabilizing.

In the past such an appeal to the great powers to arrest this flow of weaponry has not worked. Accordingly, there must now be direct action by the new countries themselves, a coming together, whatever the state of their present relations, to *reject* the weapons. (In these matters the boycott is always more effective than mere sanctions.) The poor countries should continue to speak to the rich on their sins, and the rich countries should accept their culpability in providing arms to the poor. But the poor countries must themselves directly address the problem. As the United States and the Soviet Union are told to transcend their suspicions and animosities in the interest of arms control, let the poor nations do likewise and thus attack their own arms competition. Following the 1982 United Nations Assembly session on disarmament we must see a major negotiating effort between the recipients of arms, one that might begin with a meeting of representatives of the recipient countries to discuss and publicize the problem and the effort. Such a meeting in, say, New Delhi would have a substantial persuasive value. None can doubt the tensions with which it and the ensuing negotiations would have to contend, but it is the fact of animosity and its consequences that makes the effort so important.

The two great powers (and the other industrialized countries) have not, to repeat, shown any serious intention of curbing the export of arms to the poor lands. This is partly because the economic interest of arms merchants is involved, partly because it is not to the rich countries that the damage is done. The heavy cost is to the new countries; so let them now come together and say no. Nothing could better prove that the flow of wisdom is not associated with per capita income, that it can move and needs to move in greater volume from the new to the old, from the poor to the rich.

AS ONE LOOKS at the task — controlling the arms competition between the nuclear powers, arresting the downward flow of arms from the rich to the poor, reducing the tensions and the arms race among the poor countries — one is left in little doubt as to the enormity of the task that mankind faces — that lies between the present and the hope for survival. The temptation to let it be, to expect and accept the worst, is strong. As with the subject of death itself, the mind retreats to psychological denial. This must not happen. The threat of nuclear war has brought a strong reaction in the rich countries, and the present commitment to the weapons competition and the arms culture must bring a like reaction in the poor countries. Their people are not only the prospective victims; the privation caused by the arms purchases and their crippling cost makes them the present victims as well. Let the victims and their governments respond. No form of past exploitation, imperialist or otherwise, has been so damaging or so dangerous as this.

V

Historical Process and the Rich

*T*HE NEED TO accommodate to historical process is not the problem of the poor countries alone. The economic systems of the more affluent lands are not working well; both the socialist and the capitalist countries are functioning far below their promise. In the broadest sense, this too is from an unwillingness to recognize that economic life is in a constant process of change and that failure and disappointment come when policy does not adjust thereto. In this essay I want to discuss this historical process and the problems of accommodation to change as these are manifest in the rich industrialized nations of the capitalist world today.

The transforming force, the engine of historical change in the mature nonsocialist countries, is organization. It is a force that is for all who are minimally responsive to the world around them to see. There is, first of all, the large and pervasive apparatus of the modern state. In the nonsocialist countries it can be a little larger or a trifle smaller as conservatives or liberals, Social Democrats or democratic socialists will it; but as all practical people must agree, it will continue to be very large.

Organization extends on to business firms, to the big corporations. In the United States a couple of thousand such giants supply approximately two-thirds of all private product, and there is a similar concentration in the other capitalist countries. Not everyone, of course, approves of these big firms, the multinationals so-called being viewed with particular suspicion. Nevertheless, the large corporation, including the large international corporation, is here to stay. For complex tasks and for modern international trade, in which the producer must follow his product with salesmanship and service to the ultimate customer, there is no alternative.

Where there are large corporations, there are, with the rarest exceptions, strong trade unions. These too will continue. Equally permanent fixtures on the scene are politically well-wired farm organizations, which have succeeded in having a floor placed under most agricultural prices in all the industrial countries of the nonsocialist world. And there is other business and professional organization of varying force. Finally, if less fearsome than in the past, there is OPEC, which controls or seeks to control the prices of the most important element in the world's energy supply.

All of this organization has a common purpose, one that only those powerfully persuaded by the free-enterprise mystique can deny. That is to take power away from the market and lodge it in greater or less measure in the hands of those who produce the product or service. This is a necessary, indeed an indispensable, feature of advanced economic development, a part of the historical process. Modern corporate planning requires that, to the extent possible, future prices be subject to intelligent influence, if not control; the price prospect cannot be purely random. The same is true of costs. And of the consumer response — that is what advertising and merchandising in the industrial countries are all about. The large-scale production of the twentieth century with its enormous investment and its long time horizons would be impossible were prices, costs, and sales volume left to the uninhibited and wholly unpredictable movements of the classical market. Equally it is the purpose of farmers, oil producers, trade union members, and the professions to escape from the hazards and, on occasion, cruelties of the free-enterprise system. The unfettered, untrammeled market is highly praised in the rhetoric of the rich capitalist countries; obeisance is rendered to it all over the industrial world; and, indeed, it is by no means dead. But the modern reality is a massive escape from its unpredictability. It is the unsolved and largely untackled problems of a world of great organizations that lie back of the present travail in the industrialized lands. Commitment to the mystique of the market leads to denial that massive organization has, in fact, changed anything. Government policy, accordingly, is kept appropriate to an earlier stage in the historical process. Not surprisingly it is sadly in conflict with present circumstance.

The changes brought about by organization are both internal and external. Internally there are the problems of management, bureaucracy, and the bureaucratic dynamic, which afflict both public and private organizations. These organizations expand in size in no close relation to their task; they age and frequently clone inadequacy by reproducing themselves and defining competence as whatever most resembles what is already there. Thus affected are the older corporate bureaucracies in the nonsocialist world and the even more elaborate structures of the Communist lands. It is a problem that has scarcely been touched, for it is only rarely conceded. Who would wish to say that capitalism and socialism have in common so deeply ingrained an internal flaw? Of this much more could be said; it must, however, await another occasion.

The external problem in the nonsocialist world lies in the interaction of modern organizational structures, the dynamic that causes a relentless upward pressure on costs and prices. Trade union claims and resulting settlements drive up prices; rising prices bring further trade union claims; farm prices are adjusted upward and the higher living costs act on wages; energy prices contribute to the upward spiral. All this is a visible and accepted fact of life in every industrial country. It is the modern form of inflation, the form inevitable in a world of organization. Prices can, of course, still rise as a result of the pressure of demand; but they also presently rise, and more persistently, as a result of the interacting dynamic of the prices and wages that have passed from the authority of the market to that of organization. The problem is further complicated by the way in which, most notably in the United Kingdom and the United States, the new form of inflation is being countered. This also reflects the continued commitment to the market mystique.

THERE ARE THREE WAYS and only three ways by which inflation, however induced, can be resisted in the industrial lands. The first is by government budget restraint — by a curtailment of spending and respending from publicly borrowed funds. This is fiscal policy. The second is by the curtailment of spending and respending from bank-borrowed funds. This is monetary policy. The third is by some form of direct intervention to restrain the pressure of trade union wages on corporate prices and of prices on wages, thus stopping the interacting upward spiral. This is an incomes and prices policy, or wage and price control. In an age of organization the problem lies in the choice among these three instruments of economic management and their combination in what has come to be called macroeconomic policy.

In the two English-speaking countries direct intervention on wages and prices is overtly in conflict with accepted market theology. If you believe you have a free market, obviously you cannot have intervention to restrain incomes and prices — to stop the wage/price spiral. It will be evident that the organizations to which I have just adverted have already undermined and extensively made obsolete the assumption of a free market, but it is the nature of the free-market faith that, in its devout manifestation, it can quite easily transcend circumstance.

Fiscal restraint — the need for limitations on public borrowing and spending to counter demand-induced inflation — is accepted in principle by the true free-market believer. But the powerful organizational dynamic of the modern state and the pressure of organizational power on modern government have made fiscal policy awkward, inelastic, and unpalatable. The services of the state, which are paid for by public spending, are an important part of the standard of living, and their reduction is strongly resisted. Many of these services work to take the rough edges off capitalism — to supply income, medical care, housing, and transportation to the needy — and they are thus in the interest of social tranquillity. Some, not excluding military expenditure, are powerfully defended by strong public and private organizational interests.

As this is written, the Reagan Administration in the United States is providing a classic example of the perverse tendencies of fiscal policy. It came to power with a strong avowal of its commitment to fiscal austerity and restraint, but it yielded to organized pressures for tax reduction, larger farm expenditures, and tremendously increased military spending, and it now faces the resulting

public borrowing and deficits on an unprece-
dented scale. (All of this has made some of its
economists, in one of the more spectacular dem-
onstrations of the flexibility of the official mind,
discover that the public deficit, however large,
does not cause inflation and is a quite normal
exemplification of conservative finance.)

With direct restraint on the wage/price spiral
excluded by market theology, and fiscal policy
excluded by organizational and political pressure, there remains only monetary policy. This, in
the United States as also in Britain, is the residual
legatee in the action against inflation. There is no
need, some professional vested interest of my
fellow economists apart, to make economics
more complicated than it is: nearly everything
about the economic prospect for the United
States, and by extension for much of the industrial world at large, can be understood (for so
long as it is suffered) by this commitment to
monetary policy.

MONETARY POLICY does work against inflation, is working now (in 1982) in the United
States. But it is a policy that works in the highly
organized sector of the economy only at the price
of severe pain. And while it works better in the

market sector of the economy, it is not without pain there also.

All rigorous monetarists, immune to historical process, are firm in their belief that the classical free market needed for a workable monetary policy still exists. This belief derives not from observation but from faith. When monetary policy is brought to bear in the world of strong organizations, as in the United States and Britain, it has consequences far different from what would be expected in a classical market economy. And those different circumstances are the reality of our time.

To counter inflation, monetary policy, as noted, restricts spending and respending from bank and other borrowing—the spending and respending of the money and money equivalents that are created by such borrowing. The first effect of this constraint in a highly organized economy is not, we now know, on prices but on output and employment. And before wage and price increases are curtailed, the output/employment effect must be relatively drastic. Only when there is substantial idle plant capacity, substantial unemployment, is the upward thrust of wages and prices arrested. This is not a matter of theory; it is the clear recent experience of

Britain and the clear and yet more recent experience of the United States. In other words, inflation yields to monetary policy in the modern industrial world only when the economy goes into a relatively severe recession. So long as any government relies exclusively on monetary policy to control inflation, it will succeed only as it induces a recession. If under political pressure it has to loosen the monetary restraint[1] — a more likely prospect — then inflation will resume.

But this is not all. The impact of the recession resulting from an effective monetary policy is not evenly distributed. The curtailment of bank and other lending by which monetary restraint is imposed is achieved through high interest rates — rates high enough to discourage borrowing. These high interest rates are far from neutral; those who do business on borrowed money and those who sell extensively on credit are singled out for particular punishment. In the United States the whole construction industry (particularly the housing industry), the automobile manufacturers, the farm-equipment industry, small business generally — all have suffered from mon-

---

1. As appears to have happened in the United States as this essay goes to press.

etarist constraint precisely as one would expect. The same is true in Britain. American businessmen who support the monetarist policy, as many do, are showing a remarkable, if not wholly commendable, tendency to put political ideology ahead of enlightened self-interest.

Equally evident is the international effect of reliance on monetary policy. The high interest rates recently in effect in the United States have drawn deposit funds from other countries; in doing so, they have forced the other countries to choose between a protective resort to equally high rates or some form of exchange control. So far the American monetarist policy has resulted in defensive rates in the rest of the industrial world; but it could, if it continues, lead to an individual or collective move to exchange controls and a breakup of the present international financial system.

THERE IS A further problem that darkens the picture. The Reagan Administration came to office in early 1981 with a powerful commitment to the monetarists, but Mr. Reagan also brought to Washington the economic convocation called the supply-side economists. They believed, or in any case learned, that they could win applause by avowing that if taxes on individuals and corporations are drastically reduced, production will expand, public revenues will rise, and the public sector will be as well financed as before. Taxes, in their view, are a major constraining influence on economic effort and investment, so the result of the supply-side fantasy has been large reductions in personal and corporate income taxes.

This description of the supply-side economic formula as fantasy is now widely accepted. It is visibly as well as logically impossible to combine an expansion of the economy encouraged by tax reduction with a contraction of the economy brought about by the rigorous application of monetary policy. But also, there is no evidence that past taxation in the industrial countries, including in the United States, was effectively a constraint on either business effort and initiative or investment. Because something is attractive in the rhetoric and appealing to an audience does not mean that it is effective in the statistics. The most influential economic officer in the Reagan Administration, Mr. David Stockman, the Director of the Office of Management and Budget, has called the supply-side vision simply a cover for the reduction of taxes in the upper-income tax brackets.

However, the supply-side aberration, in combination with a sharp increase in military spending, has now placed in prospect yet larger budget deficits—public borrowing on a monumental peacetime scale. This means that, for restraining inflation, there will be less rather than more reliance on fiscal policy, more rather than less reliance on monetary policy. There will be more public borrowing, with a further upward thrust in interest rates. Or, if the monetary policy is relaxed under political pressure (a development, as I have said, of no inconsiderable likelihood), then production and employment will increase but inflation will resume. The policy presently being followed in Washington does not specify continued recession. It does specify that there will be either recession or (maybe more likely) renewed inflation—perhaps even some of both. This is not a happy prospect; none other can be seriously anticipated.

WHAT IS THE HOPE for something better? The signs for which to watch are two. The first will be when the United States moves to a greater emphasis on fiscal policy and a lesser emphasis on monetary policy—something I would urge on the other industrial nations as well. Fiscal policy—a tighter budget as an instrument for controlling demand and that part of inflation which results from the pull of demand — is in every way (except in political ease) superior to monetary policy. It attacks consumption expenditure rather than investment expenditure and thus has a less damaging effect on productivity; it does not single out interest-sensitive industries for punishment; in its effect on the economy it is more predictable; it does not, as does monetary policy, encounter the principal modern difficulty of all central banks, which is in defining what money is and in controlling with precision what cannot be defined. With stronger fiscal policies the governments of all the industrial countries can proceed toward narrower budget deficits (or their elimination), lower interest rates, and easier lending conditions. It is especially urgent that the United States move decisively in this direction. There is room for political preference in how the American deficit is reduced. I have urged canceling the proposed 1983 personal-income-tax reductions, withdrawing the corporate-income-tax concessions that were enacted in 1981, and taking a stern look at military expenditures. This last point, as these essays have sufficiently argued, goes beyond economics to the issue of arms control and survival itself.

The other signal for change will be the adoption

by all the industrial countries of deliberate and specific incomes and prices policies. Germany, Austria, Switzerland, other European states, and Japan have largely accepted the necessity for them. Wage settlements in those countries are adjusted to what can be afforded from current prices. Britain and the United States, deterred by a much more retarded commitment to classical economic ideology, are the laggard cases. An incomes and prices policy accommodates to the logic of an economy in which large business and labor organizations have gained the power to press wage and price claims and thus to bring about the interacting upward spiral of wages and prices. Monetary and fiscal policy arrest this spiral only as they arrest growth and expansion and produce instead a recession. This, again, is not a matter of theory but of stern British and American experience.

Direct restraint on wages and prices in the highly organized sector of the economy takes the burden of inflation control off monetary and fiscal policy and allows the economy to operate at more nearly full employment, more nearly full capacity, and with the growth and expansion that then result. This policy is not a radical step into the unknown; as noted, it is already a part of the economic management of many of the industrial countries. It is an inevitable accommodation to the highly organized economies of our time. Much argument to the contrary, a strong incomes and prices policy served the United States well during the Second World War; there is no memory of inflation from that period. It served again in the Korean War; yet again in more informal fashion in the Kennedy years; and for Richard Nixon. By the time of the election in 1972 such a policy, the handiwork of stalwart conservatives, had brought unemployment down to 5 percent of the labor force and the inflation rate to less than 4 percent per annum. Each time, inflation resumed when the controls were lifted, but it is surely not an argument against a policy that it does not work when you do not have it. The logic of an incomes and prices policy is confined to the highly organized sector of the economy where historical process — industrial and trade union concentration and their pattern-setting effects — has made it necessary and where, it should be noted, that same concentration — a few thousand corporations, a few hundred labor contracts — makes it administratively possible.

I do not suggest that wage and price restraint will be either pleasant or easy; good economic management is always an exercise in hard choices. I do suggest that it is far superior, in the most conservative sense, to price stability achieved, as now, through extensive unemployment and

widely distributed business suffering and failure
— to the control of incomes and prices by gross
hardship, with inflation as the alternative. The
adoption of a wage/price policy by the United
States will be a major turning point in the world
economic prospect; no one should expect such a
turning point until such a policy is in effect. All the
alternatives to it lower inflation by depressing the
economy and sacrificing growth — or they accept
continuing inflation.

No one will see all this as an exercise in opti-
mism, but there is one glimmer of light. The
controlling influence in economic policy, as in-
creasingly we realize, is not ideology but hard
historical circumstance. Not even the most committed ideologist can resist history in an enduring
way if the suffering is sufficiently great. The day
will come when the monetarist and associated
classical-market fantasies will fade, and we will
discover that it is better to adjust to the modern
world — that of great corporations, strong trade
unions, a large government apparatus, and the
other manifestations of organization in our time.
Then we will have industrial economies that will
work, not as they do at present but as they should
and must.

I COME to the end of these lectures — essays, as I
now make bold to call them. No one will doubt

the depth and diversity of the tasks that performance in the rich lands, progress in the poor lands,
and the survival of both rich and poor entail. It
would be easy for us to surrender to pessimism; as
always, that has an aspect of hard-headed practi-
cality. We must not. We must keep alive the
thought that salvation is possible. It is to this end
that these essays are directed. I plead with all who
encounter them for active, effective effort. Books
can point the way; things happen when readers
join the march.

Index

Afghanistan, Soviet Union and, 32, 39, 43
Africa: economic plans for new states, 6, 8, 22; imperialism in, 27, 28, 38, 40
Albania, 30, 31
Algeria, Soviet aid to, 30, 31
Angola, MPLA regime, 32
Arms race, *see* Military power
Asia: economic plans for new states, 6; imperialism in, 28, 29, 40
Austria, 79
AWACS, 58. *See also* Military power

Ben Bella, Ahmed, 30, 31
Boulanger, Georges Ernest, 15
Brandt Commission, 15, 57n4
Brazil, 36
Britain, 15; imperialism, 26, 37, 38, 39; arms sales, 47, 57n4; arms expenditures–GNP ratio, 54; inflation, 69; monetary policy, 72–75, 79
Bulgaria, 29–30
Bureaucracies, 9, 48, 52, 68

Canada, education, 18–19n3
Capital investment, 67; as instrument of progress, 8, 10–13, 17, 18, 22; political and cultural development vs, 11–12, 17, 22; military vs civilian, 15; vs technical training/education, 17, 18, 22;

postwar, in Europe and Japan, 35; arms expenditures vs nonmilitary, 56
Capitalism: and economic development, 9, 10–11; and bureaucracy, 9; socializing effect, 10; as "threat," 28, 50; flaws in/failure of, 31, 65, 69; choice between Communism and, 41; effect of nuclear conflict, 51; and corporations, 66; free market and, 68; state services and, 71
CENTO, 33, 34
China, 34, 43; Russian technicians in, 21, 60; relations with Soviet Union, 21, 29–30, 31, 33, 60; and UN, 33; war with India (1962), 59
Civil War, U.S., 12, 15
Communism, 40; as "threat," 28, 30–31, 50; expansion, 29–30, 32; choice between capitalism and, 41; effect of nuclear conflict, 51; bureaucracies under, 68
Constitutional government (Latin America), 14
Corporations, 66, 81; and corporate bureaucracy, 9, 68; and corporate planning, 67
Costa Rica, 14
Costs: control of/pressures on, 67, 69. *See also* Prices
Cromwell, Oliver, 15
Cuba, 33, 40; and Angola, 32

83

Index

Cultural development: capital investment vs, 11–12, 33; and economic development, 16–21; requirements, 21–22

Czechoslovakia, 29

Decolonization, see Imperialism

Democracy: military power vs, 14–15; education and, 19; U.S. commitment to, 35; irrelevance to nuclear survivors, 51

Developed countries, 2

Dominican Republic, U.S. troops in, 39

Dulles, John Foster, 33

Duvalier, François, 33

Eastern Europe: affluence, 3; Communist states, 29–30; Soviet influence, 39

East Germany, 29

Economic development: as historical process of change, 4, 8–9, 10, 23–24, 41, 51, 65, 67, 80, 81; as sign of progress, 7–8, 10–11; complexity, 9, 23–24; social requirements, 20; power of producer (vs market) as feature, 67

Education: economic development and, 8, 11–12, 13, 16–21; free and compulsory, 8, 11, 18–19; capital investment vs, 17, 18, 22; general vs technical, 17, 18, 20–21; importance, 17, 18–19, 22; and culture of poverty, 18–19; discipline and, 19–20

Egypt: Soviet advisers, 21, 30, 31, 60; wars with Israel, 59

Eisenhower, Dwight D., 48, 49

Employment/unemployment, 73, 77, 79, 80

Encirclement, 33

Energy prices, 69. See also Prices

Ethiopia, 10, 32

Eurocommunism, 31

Europe, antinuclear political movement, 53

"Expansionism," 27

Falkland Islands, 35

Farming: technical skills and, 20–21; and farm organizations, 66; and farm prices, 66, 69; and farm policy, 71

Feudalism, 28

Fiscal policy/restraint, 70, 71, 72, 77, 79; superiority, 77–78

France, 15, 31; Communist party, 31; imperialism, 37, 38, 43; arms sales, 47, 57n4

Free enterprise: as "solution," 7, 41; "defense" of, 50; organization vs, 67–68

Free market: commitment to mystique of, 7, 68, 69, 70–71, 73, 81; unpredictability, 67–68; and fiscal restraint, 70–71; and wage/price intervention, 70

Germany: unification, 12; arms expenditures–GNP ratio, 54–55, 56; nonmilitary investment–GNP ratio, 56; incomes and prices policy, 79

Ghana, 31

Government policy: conflict with present circumstance, 68; against inflation, 70, 74; organizational pressures and, 71, 72. See also Inflation

Index

Communism, 31; rich coexistence with (vs domination of), 44; self-determination, 44–45; effect of arms race on, 46–47; weapons flow to, 47, 56–64; need for rejection of weapons, 62–63, 64

Portuguese empire, 37, 38

Poverty: Christian tradition of, 1, 18; national, vs personal wealth, 1–2; culture of, 17–19; Communism and socialism as "solutions," 31, 32

Prices: influences on/control of, 66, 67, 69, 72, 73; farm, 66, 69; oil, 67; energy, 69; incomes and prices policy, 70, 79–81

Production/productivity, 67; economic, military expenditure vs, 54–56; in U.S., 66, 76, 77; fiscal policy effect on, 78

Public borrowing/deficit, 70, 71, 72, 77

Reagan, Ronald, and Reagan Administration, 27, 71, 75–77

Recession, 74, 77, 79

Rich/industrial countries: terminology for, 1–2; advice from poor countries, 3, 5, 24, 25, 61, 62–63; agreement on economic matters, 6–7, 9; economic development history, 8, 11, 12, 15, 23, 41, 50; arms sales, 15; misunderstanding of cultural development process, 16; technical training by, 17; relations with new nations, 21, 46; effect of assistance to poor countries, 22; newly developed, 36; coexistence with poor (vs domination of), 44; failure of economic systems, 65; advertising and merchandising, 67; inflation remedies, 70; economic prospect, 72; incomes and prices policies, 79

Rumania, 29, 31

Rusk, Dean, 30

Russian empire, 37

Russian Revolution, 12

Saudi Arabia, aircraft for, 57–58

SEATO, 33, 34

Singapore, 20, 43

Sivard, Ruth Leger, 54–55

Social Democrats, 66

Socialism: and economic development, 6, 9–10, 11, 65, 69; as "solution," 6–7, 31, 41; administrative needs, 9–10; Marx's view, 10; rejection of, 32; as "threat," 50; effect of nuclear conflict, 51

Somalia, 32

Somoza regime, 33

South Vietnam, U.S. and, 36, 39, 42–43, 58–59

South Yemen, 32

Soviet Union: influence, 4, 39, 40, 42; economic development advice, 6–7, 8; arms sales/aid, 15, 30, 57n4, 60; exported technical skills, 21, 30, 31, 60; relations with China, 21, 29–30, 31, 33, 60; relations with U.S., 25, 34, 44, 46–52; as imperial power, 25, 27, 28, 29–32, 33, 34, 36, 39–40, 43, 44; arms competition with U.S., 46–56, 61, 62, 63; risk of nuclear conflict, 51;